ADVERTISING FOR DECORATORS

HOW TO ATTRACT BETTER CUSTOMERS AND INCREASE PROFITS

By

JON MEARS

Copyright © 2020

www.jmears.co.uk

Introduction

This book has been written to help you advertise your business and services in the best possible way.

A lot of decorators believe that advertising is something you only need to do when you're just starting out. Or as a last resort if you're having a quiet spell.

They believe that once you're up and running, you shouldn't *need* to advertise. And that your reputation alone should be enough to guarantee you more than enough work.

I'm sure you've heard the following phrase more than once:

'I don't need to advertise; all my work comes from word of mouth'

Perhaps you've even said it yourself?

Yes, a good reputation can be more than enough to keep you busy. But advertising is not just about keeping you busy. Good advertising will mean you attract better customers. The sort of customers who not only pay more, but they value your skills more. This means you will be happier and more fulfilled in your work.

Good advertising also means you only need to do the sort of work you really enjoy.

You might love painting kitchens and hate doing exterior work. However, to make sure you're always busy you advertise that you do all types of decorating. This means in the summer you end up doing several weeks of exterior work that you really don't enjoy.

If you were good at advertising, you would never need to do an exterior job again. You could just do kitchen refurbishments every week.

When you think about it like this, I'm sure you'll agree that any painter and decorator can benefit from learning how to advertise effectively.

This book will cover everything you need to know about creating adverts that bring in the right sort of business.

I'll guide you through all the different types of advertising, from leaflets and business cards, to videos and case studies.

This book is not written to be read once and then discarded. It is written to be a reference book for whenever you need it.

Whenever you find yourself designing something to attract new customers, whether it be a social media post or a new advert for the local parish magazine, you can pick this book up and find the chapter that helps.

If you are a painter and decorator with any of the following goals, this book can help you:

- Start your own business
- Grow your existing business
- Target a different type of work
- Specialise in a certain type of work (E.G uPVC spraying or kitchen repainting)
- Increase profits
- Work for customers who value you more
- Increase the value of your business so you can sell it
- Work fewer hours
- Take on more staff
- Stop being a busy fool and start earning some proper money

So, if you're ready to say goodbye to those dreaded quiet spells and say hello to smashing your business goals, then let's get started!

Table of Contents

Introduction

Table of Contents

Legal Notes

Chapter 1. Leave your ego at the door

Chapter 2. Creating a swipe file

Chapter 3. Choose your niche

Chapter 4. Identify your perfect customer

Chapter 5. The benefits of paid advertising

Chapter 6. Keep your message simple

Chapter 7. Headlines

Chapter 8. Images

Chapter 9. Bullet points

Chapter 10. How to write the perfect sales document. Every time.

Chapter 11. Advertising by post

Chapter 12. Business cards

Chapter 13. Your website

Chapter 14. Case studies

Chapter 15. Email marketing

Chapter 16. Social media advertising

Chapter 17. Advertising in print

Chapter 18. Blogs

Chapter 19. Video

Conclusion

About The Author

Legal Notes

First published in the United Kingdom in 2020

Copyright © Jon Mears

Jon Mears has asserted his right to be identified as the author of this work in accordance with the Copyright, Designs and Patents Act 1988

All rights reserved. No part of this publication may be reproduced, stored in a retrieval system, or transmitted in any form or by any means, electronic, mechanical, photocopying, recording or otherwise, without prior permission of the copyright owner.

This book is not intended to provide personalised legal, financial, or investment advice.

The Author and Publisher specifically disclaim any liability, loss or risk which is incurred as a consequence, directly or indirectly of the use and application of any contents of this work.

Great care has been taken to ensure all facts and quotes are accurate at the time of writing.

Opinions expressed are solely my own and do not express the views or opinions of my employer.

First edition

December 2020

Chapter 1. Leave Your Ego at the Door

Advertising is about generating business.

More business, better quality business and more predictable business.

And any company worth its salt should be doing it. All. The. Time.

For some reason, a lot of tradesmen look down on other trade companies who advertise.

They think that if you're truly good at what you do, you shouldn't need to advertise.

In my humble opinion, this is a load of rubbish.

Apple are really good at making phones and laptops, yet they still advertise. McDonalds are pretty good at making burgers and they still advertise. Coca Cola, Samsung, Tesco, you name any big and successful company. They all advertise.

So why shouldn't you?

The other thing to remember is that advertising is not about showing the world how clever you are.

All too often people over complicate their message and pretend to be something they are not.

Small companies always seem to pretend they are bigger than they really are.

You've seen the adverts before:

'Our staff are all fully qualified and have an impeccable eye for detail'

Our staff?

You're a sole trader. Give it a rest mate.

People tend to use long and over complicated words that they would never use in real life, because they want to seem intelligent and professional.

All these things simply distract from what your company is really about, and to be honest, probably do more harm than good.

A question I like to ask painters and decorators whenever I meet them is:

'Why do your customers choose you over anyone else?'

Do you know what 99% of them answer?

They choose them because of who they are. Their personality. The rapport they built up when they first met.

That's what makes them unique. The person behind the company.

Not the fact that they are time served and have 30 years' experience in the trade.

And yet, when it comes to writing an advert about their business, people always seem to write the same boring and generic rubbish that everyone else writes.

Because that's what you're supposed to do, right?

That's what the big companies do. So that's what you should do?

Wrong.

Big companies have big budgets. They can afford to run advertising campaigns to 'increase brand awareness'.

You are a small company. You have a small budget. And there is nothing wrong with that. Don't let your ego get in the way of what you are trying to do with your advertising.

You shouldn't be trying to copy big companies.

They have very different objectives to you.

Big companies will spend millions on making adverts that look cool and improve their brand image.

This is not what you are trying to achieve as a small business.

You are trying to find your next job so that you can pay your mortgage.

Remember this whenever you are advertising.

If you let your ego get in the way and you pretend to be a bigger company that you really are, then all that will happen is you waste valuable time and money.

Listen, I'll admit I have been just as bad as the next person for all of this stuff.

I've written adverts and sent emails to people that would suggest the company I worked for was an absolute giant.

When the reality was that I was sat in a tiny little office with two other people. And the 'board room' at our 'Head quarters' was more like a cupboard in a portacabin.

I've spent money on making flashy videos and brochures that made no impact on sales.

I've then tried convincing my boss that the campaign hadn't failed, as it was all about improving 'brand image'.

Let me tell you, as a small company, when someone says the advertising campaign was all about 'getting the name out there' or 'improving brand awareness', what they really mean is…the advertising campaign bombed, and they wasted a ton of money.

I'll give you a more recent example of when I tried to make a 'cool' and 'clever' advert.

Whilst working for a paint manufacturing company, I was creating a poster style advert that could be used in stores and on social media.

The paint had been getting some good reviews from decorators and sales were growing. This was inflating my ego and I had the delusion that we were the 'best kept secret' in the paint industry.

I designed the advert as if I were launching the new iPhone.

Picture this: it was a plain white sheet of A4 paper with an image of the paint tin in the centre. Underneath was the caption:

'When you know…'

Clever right? Sounds cool, yeah?

Well I basically took the afternoon off after that. I was so proud of myself. It was simple, elegant…beautiful.

It makes me cringe now.

There were several issues with this advert, but the main problem was the caption 'When you know…'

It was supposed to be a nod to the decorators who already knew we had a good product, and it was supposed to intrigue other decorators about it.

However, the advert did absolutely nothing for sales.

I would guess that 99% of people that saw the advert probably read the caption 'When you know…' and then said to themselves…. 'Know what?' and just kept on scrolling through social media.

Not one person ever looked at that advert and said to me 'What's all this about then?'

So as cool and clever as I thought this advert was, it was a complete failure. As not only did it not produce any sales. It didn't even trigger any conversations.

The point is, that one way or another, I've learned my lessons. Ego has no place in advertising.

I've found out that the key to successful advertising is to be authentic and to be yourself. Nothing more. Nothing less.

Summary

Understand what sort of business you are and make sure you are clear on your individual goals. Don't let ego dictate your advertising tactics. Don't be tempted to copy what larger companies are doing. They have different objectives to you, and much bigger budgets. Stay true to who you are, and you'll be far more successful.

Chapter 2. Creating a swipe file

What the hell is a swipe file?

Good question. Let me tell you.

A swipe file is a collection of great adverts.

Whether that be leaflets, social media posts, magazine adverts. Anything.

To be effective in advertising you need to start building your own swipe file.

How do you do this?

Well, from now on, every time an advert catches your attention you are going to save it in a file.

So, if a social media post has a great headline that intrigues you and makes you want to read more, you need to screen shot it and save it into your personal swipe file.

If you receive a leaflet in the post or see an advert in a newspaper that makes you stop and read on you need to snap a photo of it and save it on your phone.

It might be that the headline isn't amazing, but the rest of the advert is brilliant, perhaps the text is really well written or the structure of it looks great.

Basically, if you see an advert that either catches your attention, or makes you want to buy a product or service, you need to save it in your 'swipe file'.

WHY DO YOU NEED TO DO THIS?

The simplest way to create an advert that works, is to model it on one that has already worked on you.

Notice I said 'Model' and not 'Copy'.

Modelling your advert on something is not completely straight forward though.

There are loads of different things that can make an advert successful. So, to identify what works we first need to look for patterns. This is why you need a swipe file.

Your swipe file will be an ever-evolving document. Something that you'll often update and refer back to.

As your file grows, you'll develop an understanding of the type of headlines that catch your attention. You'll learn techniques that help you write more engaging sales copy, so potential customers want to read more.

Of course, during this book we are going to try and shortcut this process. I'm going to share with you loads of techniques and tactics you can use.

However, advertising is constantly evolving. I can show you the basic techniques that have worked for decades, but by creating your own swipe file you can boost this with whatever new tactics are proving successful at the time.

As I said, advertising is constantly evolving. So, to keep on top of things, you need to keep evolving too.

When will I look at my swipe file?

If you've ever sat down to write a piece of sales copy, whether that be for a leaflet, brochure, social media post or anything really, you'll understand that knowing where to start is one of the most difficult parts of the process.

I think most people have, at one time or another, sat in front of a blank page or screen without a clue what to do.

Eyes glazed over. Seemingly nothing going on inside your head.

Having a swipe file to look at helps get your creative juices flowing.

Whenever you sit down to write and design an advert you can have a quick flick through your swipe file to get yourself in the right frame of mind and look for some inspiration.

Once your swipe file is big enough you should be able to refer to it at any given time and find everything you need to create an outstanding advert that's perfect for the situation.

You'll be able to flick through headlines that you know are great at getting the attention of customers and model your own version.

You'll be able to structure the text, so it flows brilliantly.

You'll even have loads of inspiration for how to best lay out the design. Where to put the images, where to put the text, everything!

Summary

Start putting together your own swipe file today. Create a folder on your phone or laptop where you can store every advert you see that does one of the following three things:

1. Catches your attention
2. Makes you read the whole thing
3. Makes you want to buy the product or service

Doing this will make it quicker and easier for you to create brilliant adverts forever more.

CHAPTER 3. CHOOSE YOUR NICHE

I've said it before and I'm sure I'll say it a thousand more times.

If you try to be everything to everyone, you'll end up being nothing to anyone.

Although your advert might be seen by hundreds, even thousands of people. It gets read by one person at a time.

This means, you need to write it as if you are speaking directly to one person. Your customer.

When you offer loads of services all on one advert it becomes increasingly difficult to do this.

Think about it like this:

Most potential new customers will be looking for one service. As a decorator they might want you to paint a room, hang some wallpaper, paint their kitchen cabinets or maybe spray their uPVC windows.

It is highly unlikely they will ask you to do all these things on the first visit.

So, when they look at your leaflet and it says that you offer 'interior and exterior painting, commercial and residential work, wallpapering, kitchen refurbishments and uPVC spraying.' 80% of that advert is not applicable to the person reading it.

You are not just wasting precious (and expensive) advertising space, but you are also running the risk that the customers stop reading before they get to the part they are actually interested in.

So, how do we fix this problem?

We choose a niche.

An area that we specialise in.

That might be paper hanging, commercial painting, uPVC spraying. Anything. Just make it specific.

But what if I don't want to specialise in just one thing I hear you ask.

Don't worry. You can still do all the things you already do. All we are going to do is simply change the way you advertise each service.

Instead of doing one big advert that tries to attract everyone (and often doesn't catch anyone)

We are going to do smaller advertising campaigns that are far more targeted.

For example, let's say you are doing a Facebook ad campaign.

Instead of spending £50 on adverts that tell everyone about all your services, we will instead spend £10 on an advert about uPVC spraying, £10 about wallpaper hanging and so on and so on.

Your total spend will be no different. But the results will improve massively.

At this point you may be concerned that sending all these messages might confuse potential customers.

People might wonder what exactly you do. Are you a uPVC specialist? A kitchen specialist? What!?

Don't worry. There are ways that we will manage that.

To start, if we create an advert specifically about the fact, we offer uPVC spraying as a service. We are not saying that we don't offer other types of decorating. We are simply using this advert to give you as much information about uPVC spraying as we can.

Also, when you split your advertising up like this, you will quickly find out which services are getting people's attention. You may find after 6 months that nobody enquires about your wallpaper hanging Facebook ads. So, you can cut those out and spend the extra money on the services that are generating enquiries.

Imagine a social media post as follows:

(The image is a freshly sprayed uPVC window)

Caption 1:

Have a look at this weeks' transformation!

Get your free no obligation quote from HGA Decorators TODAY

- We spray uPVC windows and doors
- Interior and exterior painting
- Wallpaper hanging
- Kitchen refurbishments
- Commercial and residential work

Caption 2:

Have a look at this weeks' transformation!

Get your free no obligation quote from HGA Decorators TODAY

- We spray uPVC windows and doors
- Using the latest spray equipment
- Super durable paints so they look great all year round
- Incredible care is taken during preparation to protect your home and ensure a perfect finish
- Far more cost effective than replacing your windows

Each of these two captions had the same image, same headline, same sub headline and the same first bullet point.

However, as you can see, caption 1 used the last 4 bullet points to give generic information about the business (this is what most adverts look like).

Caption 2 used the other 4 bullet points to reinforce the message and give more relevant information.

Seeing these two adverts next to each other you should be able to see that Caption 2 would be a lot more effective than Caption 1.

Caption 1 would likely get very little response. The advert is trying to be everything to everyone. By doing this, it doesn't really give the potential customer enough information to make any sort of decision.

Caption 2 however, is a different case. Caption 2 uses the final 4 bullet points to answer questions a potential customer might have if they are considering having their uPVC windows sprayed.

This means the customer is more well informed and far more likely to engage with you.

This is not the only advantage to choosing a niche and advertising accordingly.

When you choose a niche and advertise specifically for that, you will be seen as a specialist.

And specialists win more work and get paid more because people trust them more.

Why is this?

Think about it this way: Let's say Mrs. Jones has a nice big house with a very expensive kitchen.

She doesn't want to replace the whole kitchen, so she decides she wants it repainted and starts searching for local companies.

The first company she finds is a decorator who offers the usual services. Painting, wallpaper hanging, kitchens, interior, exterior etc.

The second company is a specialist kitchen refurbishment / painting company.

The first thing to realise, is that Mrs. Jones is far more likely to call the specialist kitchen company first because their advertising likely answers more of her questions straight away. (As we found with the 2 uPVC captions earlier)

But let's say that she gets both companies in to quote for the work.

The reality is that Mrs. Jones is far more likely to go with the specialist company. Even if they are more expensive.

In fact, she might even go for them BECAUSE they are more expensive.

Think about it.

Mrs. Jones has a very expensive kitchen; she needs to trust the company to do a great job.

Who is she going to trust more? The decorator who does the odd kitchen? Or the company that specialises in kitchens?

When you are a specialist and you are expensive, people will trust that you are very good at what you do. This means that having a niche not only means you will get more work, but you'll also get more *profitable* work.

If you owned a Rolls Royce and it broke down one day. Would you take it to Dave the local mechanic down the road who said he'll have a look at it? Or would you take it to a Rolls Royce specialist?

You know the specialist will cost more, but you trust them to do the job properly.

One other concern people tend to have when I suggest advertising your company as a specialist is that it makes it difficult to quote for different work with the same customer.

For example, you said you were a kitchen specialist but now you want to quote for a wallpapering job they have. Or a uPVC spraying job they have.

The answer to this is that you can specialise in more than one thing. It is quite reasonable for someone to have been on a furniture spraying course and a uPVC window spraying course. To me, this would qualify them as a specialist in both fields.

Also, there is no reason once you've completed the specialist job that you can't say to the customer you also offer a load of other services.

Being a specialist is about getting them to trust you straight away. Once you've done the first job for them their level of trust in you will increase and they'll be more than happy to offer you other types of work. Even if it isn't what you 'specialise' in.

If you are a larger company with a few staff members you could even train individual staff members to specialise in certain aspects of decorating. This means if the customer has a different job to quote for, you'll simply send a different staff member to do the job. Having staff trained like this is also an effective way to run your company. The staff will work more efficiently and do a better job if they are doing the same type of work every day. But that's a topic for a different book!

One more thing. If you are still not convinced you should advertise to a niche. Think about why you bought this book.

Chances are, you are a painter and decorator. The book is written specifically for painters and decorators. The advert that led you to the book was targeted to you and explained how the benefits are specific to you.

If I'd called the book 'Advertising for small businesses' or simply 'Advertising tips and techniques', would you have bought it? Would you have been as confident that it would help you specifically?

Probably not.

Summary

No matter how many thousands of people see your adverts, they are read by one person at a time. Therefore, good adverts speak to people on an individual basis. Don't write like you are the Queen addressing the nation. Write like you are speaking to a friend.

Choosing a niche and advertising accordingly will increase the amount of good quality enquiries you get.

You can specialise in a few different areas if you want to, but make sure your advertising campaigns focus on just one thing at a time.

CHAPTER 4. IDENTIFY YOUR PERFECT CUSTOMER

Once you've decided what niche or specialism you are going to advertise, you next need to decide *who* you are going to advertise it to.

Again, we must remember the saying:

If you try to be everything to everyone, you'll end up being nothing to anyone.

Not everyone is going to be a good customer for your business. Not everyone will be able to afford your services. Not everyone is going to like you.

Knowing this and understanding this is crucial to good advertising.

There is a saying I read in Jim Edwards' book 'Copywriting secrets' that I love for things like this:

'Love me or hate me, there is no money in the middle.'

Essentially, this means that you can't please everyone, nor should you even try. Because if you try to be liked by everyone, you'll end up just creating dull and generic copy that nobody cares about.

By the way, I should point out now that when I refer to 'copy' as in creating copy or writing copy. This literally just means the words you use when trying to sell something.

Sometimes I'll say copy, sometimes I'll say text. It's all the same.

Whether it is the sales copy on a leaflet, or the copy written on an email. It is all just simply my way of referring to the words you write.

Anyway, as I was saying, 'there is no money in the middle'. This is a concept that took me a long time to come to terms with.

It can be very difficult when people actively say negative things about you or your business.

This can mean that you shy away from pushing the boundaries.

But it shouldn't.

Once you embrace the fact that not everyone is going to like what you have to say, you will start writing much more engaging stuff.

This will in turn get the attention of the people you really want to speak to. Your perfect customers.

Quick Tip:

When people say negative things about you or your company it is usually on social media and it is usually them just trying to get a reaction out of you.

As hard as it is, you just need to ignore it.

If in doubt, remember these wise words from Mark Twain:

'Never argue with an idiot. They will drag you down to their level and beat you with experience'

So how do we identify our perfect customer?

Well, if you are an established company then you can look on your experience to answer this question.

Ask yourself:

Which customers did I enjoy working for the most?

Which jobs were most fulfilling?

Which jobs were the most profitable?

When you answer these questions, you'll have a good idea of your perfect customer.

If you are new to the industry, don't worry, you can still establish your perfect customer very easily.

Typically, your perfect customer will be the person who you can offer the most value to. The customer who wants exactly what you are best positioned to offer.

To find your perfect customer you must therefore understand what solutions do you offer better than anyone else? What makes you unique?

Let's say you are particularly good at kitchen repainting.

What would you perfect customer look like?

Think about some of the challenges they may have and list them out.

Challenges:

- Wants to refresh the kitchen but doesn't want the expense of a completely new one
- Doesn't understand which paints are best suited for the job
- Is unsure if repainting a kitchen will last very long. Or if it will need repainting on a regular basis
- Wants to work with a reliable tradesperson
- Not sure on how long the process will take and how much disruption it will cause

Now think about the solutions you offer and how well they resolve the customer's challenges.

Solutions:

- You can offer great savings repainting a kitchen. You have researched the cost of having a new kitchen fitted and you can explain

that the customer saves £1,000's when they choose to refurbish rather than replace
- You have thoroughly researched and personally tested numerous paints and processes to ensure you leave a flawless and highly durable finish
- You also offer a 2-year guarantee on your work and can explain to the customer the products and processes you use are designed to last for many years
- You have testimonials from customers just like them saying you completed their kitchen repainting and were seen to be trustworthy, reliable, and friendly
- You have a lot of experience painting kitchens so you can accurately estimate how long it will take to complete the job based on the size and number of units. You also have a workshop so that you can remove the cabinet doors and spray them off site. This greatly reduces disruption for the customer

A good exercise to complete would be to think of a few examples like this.

List out the potential challenges your customers have and then see how well your solutions deal with those challenges.

In the above example, if you don't know much about durable paints, or you don't have a workshop then you might not be best positioned to repaint kitchens.

This is fine.

You may be fantastic at on site spraying and you might be very fast and skilled at masking up. This could mean you are great for uPVC window spraying.

As soon as you find what you are best at, and what you enjoy doing the most, you can then start to identify your perfect customer and start serving them at the highest possible level.

When you find a customer, who is a perfect match for your business and your particular set of skills, you will be more fulfilled in your work, you will be more valued by your customers and you will also make more money.

Finding Your Perfect Customer

Now you know what your perfect customer looks like. You need to work out where to find them.

I go into some detail on this in my first book 'Sales & Marketing for Decorators', so I won't go over old ground too much now. I will instead give you the basics.

To find your perfect customer you must first work out their characteristics.

To help with this, we create something called an Ideal Customer Profile (ICP). This is also often referred to as a persona or avatar.

It helps to give your ICP a name. So, as an example, let's stick with the kitchen repainting situation and call our ICP 'Grace'.

Now let's build a profile for our imaginary 'Grace' based on what we think the characteristics of our perfect customer might be.

NB: If you are a more established company, you can draw on your experience here. Think about all your best customers and work out what they had in common.

Grace:

- 55 years old, married with 2 grown up children
- Owns a 3-bed detached house
- Very house proud
- Lives in an affluent village where the average house price is £350,000
- Enjoys playing golf and also socialising with friends at the local coffee shop

This information might seem very basic, but it does two key things for us:

1. We now have some great specifics we can use when targeting our adverts. We know what sort of houses to drop leaflets through and in which villages. We know where Grace spends time

on a weekend. We know roughly how old she is and her gender. This means we can use targeted ads on social media platforms like Facebook.

2. In Chapter 3 I said that although your adverts might be seen by hundreds, even thousands of people, they get read by one person at a time. And that means you need to write as if you are speaking directly to one person. Your customer.

    Well, that customer is 'Grace'. Now we have a clear idea on who that 'one person' is. We can confidently aim all our advertising as if we are speaking directly to 'Grace'.

Summary

Identifying your perfect customer and knowing where to find them is key to a successful and fulfilling business.

Take the time to understand what is unique about you and your business. Then work out what type of customer you can serve the best.

Once you know these things you can target your advertising accordingly. This means you will only attract the attention of good quality and profitable customers.

Chapter 5. The benefits of paid advertising

There are two types of advertising space in the world. Paid and free.

Paid advertising includes things like leaflets, newspaper ads and targeted social media campaigns.

Free advertising includes general social media, word of mouth / referrals, certain email campaigns and so on.

Most people think that free advertising is the best form of advertising, because… well, because it's free.

However, as a general rule, you should always aim to have at least 5 advertising streams.

And 2 or 3 of them should be paid advertising.

Why should you do this?

Because paid advertising forces you to focus on your 'Return on Investment' (ROI).

ROI, for those who don't know, is essentially the measure of how much money you have to spend on advertising to get some business.

If you spend £100 on an advert and get 2 customers that make you a profit of £500. You have a positive ROI of £400.

However, if you spend £100 on an advert and only get 1 customer and you only make £50 profit from them, your advert has a negative ROI of -£50.

People like free advertising because you always have a positive ROI. Afterall, you're not paying anything out. So, any business that comes in didn't cost you anything to acquire.

So how does focusing on your ROI help you in advertising?

Firstly, when you start spending money on advertising it quickly sharpens your mind and your focus.

You don't want to waste the money, so you try harder. You spend more time creating the advert and you take more care on it.

You also get lots of valuable data which you can use to improve all your advertising. Including the free stuff.

A lot of people see advertising as an artform. Something only creative people can do.

Whilst it might help to be creative. I believe advertising is more a science. Something you can continually improve by experimenting and measuring results.

This is where the data from paid advertising comes in.

Let's take the example of a paid social media campaign.

When you pay for an advert on social media you get loads of valuable data.

You can see exactly how much money you've spent, how many people viewed your advert, how many people clicked on it and so on.

You can then record this data, tweak the advert and run it again.

If the changes result in more clicks for less money, which then leads to more business, then you keep the changes. If it doesn't then you revert back to the old advert and tweak something else.

This testing is what makes the difference between good advertising and great advertising.

Often, companies will run two adverts alongside each other with just one small difference.

This is referred to as A/B testing. Or split testing.

A typical example would be trying two different headlines.

It is not uncommon for a different headline to produce results that increase sales by 10x.

(This is why I'm dedicating an entire chapter specifically to writing headlines later in the book.)

Of course, you must remember you can only test one thing at a time. Otherwise you won't know which change caused the difference in results.

So, they key is to carry out your testing on a small scale. Then once you have optimised the advert, you roll it out to the masses.

This doesn't have to be restricted to social media.

Let's say you are planning a postal campaign where you will be printing and sending 10,000 leaflets.

The best way to do this would be to test different leaflets on a small scale before printing the full 10,000 leaflets.

It doesn't need to be complicated.

You could simply try different headlines.

Imagine if you tried 5 headlines. The rest of the leaflet is identical, but there are 5 versions of headline.

You print 100 copies of each headline and distribute the flyers.

NB: You'll need a way to identify each flyer when the customer enquires with you. A reference code is a good way to do this.

It would not be uncommon to find that one of your flyers massively outperforms the others.

You may find that 4 of your headlines get about a 1% response rate, but one of them gets a 5% response rate.

How valuable is this data to your business? It's huge!

Imagine you didn't do the test and you ended up using a headline that had a 1% response rate.

You would have got 100 enquiries from your 10,000 leaflets.

But if you'd had gone with the 5% response rate headline you would have got 500 enquiries from your 10,000 leaflets.

KNOWING WHEN TO PULL THE PLUG

Most advertising campaigns don't produce the results you want. This is fine. It is all part of the process. The key is to avoid losing money by knowing when to 'pull the plug'.

Ending an advertising campaign early can be difficult to do.

Afterall, you've spent a lot of effort creating the advert and setting it all up.

You were so sure it was going to be a success.

However, learning to cut your losses is a discipline you must learn.

You'll tell yourself all sorts of things to avoid cutting an advert:

'One more day and the results will come'

'It's good for brand awareness if nothing else'

You need to block out that voice in your head. Cut your losses and move on quickly.

Of course, by testing out adverts on a small scale we are limiting our losses substantially, but this doesn't guarantee that every advert will be a success.

Knowing how to recognise a failing advert and being disciplined enough to stop spending money on it is a vital skill in advertising. One that you must strive to master.

SUMMARY

You should aim to have multiple advertising streams for your business as it'll mean you are much more secure.

A good proportion of those advertising streams should be paid for.

Paid advertising makes you focus on ROI which benefits everything you do.

Be sure to continuously test and tweak your advertising. Your campaigns should be ever evolving and improving. Advertising is as much a science as it is a creative thing.

Learn to know when to 'Pull the plug'. Don't get too attached to your creations. Treat your adverts as a means to an end.

And that end is making money.

If you're advertising is not making you money, pull the plug and try something different.

Chapter 6. Keep your message simple

Something that has taken me a long time to learn is to write like I speak.

When it comes to writing sales copy, whether that be for an email or a brochure, something strange happens to most people.

They suddenly start writing all posh. They use long words they'd never use in real life. They say things like 'therefore' and 'hence'.

Writing sales copy is not supposed to be 'fine writing'.

Sales copy is about delivering a message in simple terms, so that your target can understand it and wants to buy whatever you're selling.

As an example, let's imagine we are writing a short social media advert about uPVC window spraying.

Option 1:

Here at HGA decorators we are fully trained and qualified in uPVC spraying. Using the latest technology and 2 pack paint systems we achieve a durable and flawless finish.

To get a free, no obligation quote, call on 0121…

Option 2:

Do you want grey windows like that nice house down the street?

HGA Decorators can spray your existing windows that colour for a fraction of the cost of replacing them.

Plus, our work is guaranteed to last. (Even when the window cleaner leans his ladder against it!)

To get a quote, call Alexander on 0121…

PS: The colour you've seen is probably Anthracite grey. Click this link to see some local houses we've done in that colour.

Option 1 is how most adverts are written. Yes, it is professional. But my God is it dull.

Plus, every other advert sounds exactly the same.

How are you going to stand out and grab people's attention if you create adverts that look the same as everyone else's?

The trick is to be yourself. Write how you would talk to a potential customer. Or a friend.

The second caption is my personal twist on how I'd write that advert. It might not be your cup of tea. It might not work for your business.

The point is that at least you can tell there is some personality about it.

If I put that advert out, at least I would know that anyone who called me is definitely my sort of customer. They probably share my sense of humour and general world view that things don't need to be taken so seriously.

What I'm saying is that you don't need to write like you're back at school and taking an English exam.

Inject some personality into it.

Your personality! (Which hopefully is the same personality as your company)

BE CONCISE

Let me be clear, being concise does not necessarily mean that your adverts need to be short.

You can write 10 pages of concise information. I'd like to think this whole book is concise. It should say what it needs to say and nothing more.

Being concise is about getting rid of anything that doesn't serve your purpose.

When writing sales copy and adverts your purpose is to sell.

The more you waffle on about stuff that isn't relevant, the more likely the person is to stop reading what you've got to say.

A good process to use when trying to be concise is as follows:

1. Write your sales copy. Write without interruption and don't edit as you go along.
2. Don't look at what you've written. Walk away for a couple of hours or preferably leave it overnight.
3. Come back to what you've written and try to cut down the amount of words by half, WITHOUT losing the core message of what you've written.

You might not always be able to edit the text down this much but if you aim for half then you'll do a pretty good job in most situations.

Summary

Writing sales copy is not fine writing. It doesn't need to be difficult. Just write how you speak, avoid blabbering on, use some personality and you'll be ok. Oh, but do use a spelling and grammar checker!

Chapter 7. Headlines

Did you know headlines are read by 5x more people than the rest of the text?

You'll also remember me telling you that by simply changing your headline it has been known to increase sales by 10x.

In short, being able to write good headlines is important.

Very important.

So, what makes a good headline?

Well, first we need to understand the job of the headline.

Usually, the headline is purely about getting the attention of your perfect customer.

However, sometimes you also need the headline to do a bit of selling too.

Afterall, if 5x more people read the headline than the main body of text then you will often want to do a bit of selling in it.

It'll mean you reach a lot more people.

If by this point, you're saying to yourself:

'I don't really write headlines'

The I'm afraid you're mistaken.

Every leaflet you've ever designed, every newspaper ad, every email you've ever sent and every social media post you've ever created had a headline.

If it didn't, then that's probably why it didn't get much attention.

Now we know that you need good headlines for successful advertising, let me give you my tips for writing them.

Take your time

Most people spend hardly any time on the headline. They just start writing the advert. Sometimes it is just an afterthought.

Now that you know how much influence a good headline can have on your business you need to start giving it the time and respect it deserves.

A good rule to use is to record how long it takes you to write the main body of the text and then spend half that amount of time again on just the headline.

For example:

If you spend 30 minutes writing a sales email, you should spend a further 15 minutes creating the best subject line or headline you can.

This tip alone could make you thousands in extra profits every year.

I would guess 99% of people don't give headlines the time and respect they deserve. If you do this, you'll stand out straight away.

Keep them short(ish)

Headlines shouldn't be too long. Under 16 words is good. Under 12 is better. 9 is often said to be the sweet spot.

Remember what we said about being concise. That is your goal here.

Don't use 2 words when 1 will do.

Remember to write like you are speaking to one person

We covered this in detail in the last chapter, so I won't go over it again. Just make sure you don't forget that your headlines get read by one person at a time. Also, remember to write like you speak. Keep it friendly and conversational.

Don't put a full stop at the end of your headline

You want people to naturally flow on to the next line. If you don't believe this is a good tip, try and find a headline in a newspaper that has a full stop.

4 TYPES OF HEADLINE THAT YOU CAN USE TO MODEL YOUR OWN, AND 1 THAT YOU DEFINITELY SHOULDN'T

'HOW TO'

It is said that if you start with the words 'How to' it is almost impossible to write a bad headline.

I think this might well be true.

Think about all those classic headlines

How to lose weight

How to make money trading stocks

How to find the girl of your dreams

To beef up 'How to' headlines it is good to add a time frame and deal with a common objection.

I'll do it to the above 3 examples to show you what I mean.

How to lose 10lbs in 10 days without giving up alcohol

How to make money TODAY by trading stocks, without using your own cash

How to find the girl of your dreams in 21 days without paying for costly dating websites

See how the model works?

How to + time frame + manage common objection = Great headline.

LIST HEADLINES

'5 secrets decorators don't want you to know'

This is a classic style of headline. You can use any number. 21 tips…15 tricks….9 hacks.

Basically, it is just teasing some information your target customer might want to know.

Bonus tip: For some reason, odd numbers perform better than even. So always make it 5,7,9 etc.

STORY BASED HEADLINES

This type of headline works by capturing the emotions

These are tougher to write but can be insanely powerful. The most famous example is:

'They laughed when I sat down at the piano…but when I started to play'

I don't really need to explain why this headline is probably the most famous ever to be written.

It makes you feel the emotion of people laughing at you, then the emotion of proving them wrong…or not? There is also an element of intrigue.

Anyone who reads a headline like this and is not interested in reading the next few lines must be mental.

Just so you know, the man in the headline played beautifully and the advert was selling music lessons.

THE PROBLEM HEADLINE

Do you suffer with indigestion?

Do you hate public speaking?

Does your tired old kitchen embarrass you in front of guests?

Starting with a problem your target customer may have is a great way to catch their attention.

It is a simple template. Simply ask if they have a problem you know you can solve.

THE ONE TO AVOID

There is a type of headline that you will probably recognise which almost never produces good results.

THE 'BAIT AND SWITCH' HEADLINE

Most of these headlines will say something like:

'SEX…

…now I have your attention, let me talk to you about the benefits of our latest toaster'

Basically, they grab your attention with something you don't expect to see (the bait) and then start talking to you about something completely different (the switch).

There are occasions that this style has produced results. Usually they are 'bait and switch' images though. Rather than headlines.

For example, some historical car adverts have been run where one advert had an image of just the car and the other advert had an image of the car with a half-naked lady draped across the front.

The body of the text made no reference to the attractive woman. It purely mentioned the usual boring stuff like miles to the gallon. However, the advert with the half-naked lady outperformed the one without.

Nowadays, people are far too wise to this sort of rubbish. So, I wouldn't bother.

The chances of you pulling it off are next to zero, and all you end up doing is annoying people.

SUMMARY

Headlines are quite possibly the most important thing in advertising. If there is one thing that can have the biggest impact on the success of your advertising campaign (and the money you make) it is good quality headlines.

Give them the time and respect they deserve. Never rush a headline.

Use proven templates to increase the chances of success and don't be afraid to change and tweak headlines if an advert isn't performing.

Changing the headline of a poor performing advert is the quickest and easiest way to increase profits.

Even if the ad is doing well, you should still test different headlines as it could become even better.

Chapter 8. Images

Next to headlines, a perfectly chosen photograph, sketch or graphic can be a brilliant weapon in the fight to get your customer's attention.

For me, this is the main purpose of an image in an advert. Hooking the customer in. Getting their attention.

There is a secondary purpose of the image. And that is to show the customer a little bit about what benefit you can bring to their lives.

But for me, this is slightly less important, because the main text of the advert is going to explain that to them.

Fortunately for painters and decorators, you should never be short of a good photo to use.

Before and after photos are probably the most powerful images you can use in advertising. You see them everywhere. Weight loss transformations, make up tutorials, stain removal adverts etc.

As a painter and decorator, you can get a great before and after shot for every job you do.

So, as an industry, you have a massive advantage.

Now, I have already covered the importance of good photography for a painter and decorator in my first book 'Sales & Marketing for Decorators' but it is important enough that I need to list out the basics again here.

So, here are 12 tips on how to take better photos as a decorator:

1. Shoot into the corner of a room to make the space look bigger and to use the natural lines of the room to lead the eye into the centre of the shot.
2. Height is important. Take your shots from about mid-height. Try to capture equal amounts of ceiling and floor in the frame. Make sure all your images are from this height. Consistency is key. For most people the correct height will be around their belly button. So just remember that!
3. Tidy up! There is nothing worse than seeing charging cables hanging out or tools in the background. Imagine you're trying to get the perfect image to go on the front cover of a magazine.
4. If possible, only use natural light. Turn off all other light sources. This will give you better colours and highlights.
5. Experiment with angles. Take a few shots from each corner of the room and see what looks best.
6. Don't abuse the 'wide angle'. These types of shots can look great, but they often distort the

image and make the whole room look very odd.
7. Keep your lines straight. Use uprights and doors to ensure all lines in your image are straight. If you go to the camera settings on your phone you can turn on a grid. I'd recommend doing this as it helps you line everything up.
8. Photograph the room, not just your work. It's tempting just to capture an image of your work, but photos need context. A picture of a feature wall taken from straight on very rarely makes a good photo. You need to imagine you are showing off the whole room. It'll make the photo more interesting and more appealing to the eye.
9. Mix it up with close detail shots. Don't be afraid to get a little artsy! Experiment with close ups on certain features.
10. Zoom with your feet. If you want to zoom in on a shot, try to avoid using the zoom function on the phone. It's just not as good as actually walking forwards a few steps.
11. Edit all your photos! Before you post a photo, just take a couple of minutes to tweak the basics. Brightness, contrast, saturation etc. There are loads of free apps you can do this on, and it makes a big difference. So, make sure you do it.

12. Clean your lens! Please give the back of your phone a wipe before taking photos. Not doing that can ruin all the hard work above!

Bonus tip:

Please make sure you take your before and after photos from the same position each time. When you take a before photo from one angle and the after photo from a completely different angle it makes it harder to appreciate the full transformation. So, do yourself a favour and before you start taking those lovely 'after' photos, have a quick look at the 'before' images and remind yourself where to stand so you get the same angle.

In 99% of cases, I would recommend you use 'before and after' photos in your advertising as they are brilliant at catching people attention and showing exactly how you can help your customers.

However, on occasion, you will want to use something else.

A standalone 'After' photo of a job can often work well but if you are not showing a transformation you must make sure the photo is really good at getting people's attention and can still tell a story.

If your advert is in your leaflet or brochure you could quite easily use photos you've taken yourself. However, if your advert is in a magazine then you will be alongside lots of other adverts that are trying to get people's attention. So, if you want to win this battle, you'll need to have the best quality photograph possible.

If you're good at photography you can use your own photos, but if you're not, then you should consider using stock images.

You can get fantastic stock photos of pretty much anything nowadays. Just search for it on Google and you'll have endless options.

Some you will have to pay for, but often they are not very expensive.

There are some great free stock photo websites available. At time of writing pixabay.com is completely free and has a huge range of great quality images. So be sure to check that out.

There is also a second benefit to using stock photo websites.

When you search through stock photo websites for the perfect image you might scroll through hundreds of great quality images.

But the odd photo will stand out.

And if a photo stands out amongst a website of great photos, then you know that image is going to work brilliantly at getting the attention of your target customers.

Which is exactly what you want.

Summary

Good quality images are crucial to getting the attention of potential customers.

Take the time to learn a little bit about photography, as the photos you take will directly impact the success of your advertising. Which then affects the overall success of your business.

If you don't have the right photo for the advert, try using stock photos. You can get some great images for free or very little cost.

Chapter 9. Bullet Points

Yes, just like 'Headlines' I am dedicating an entire chapter to 'Bullet Points'. They are *that* important.

Nearly every successful advert you create will have bullet points in it.

We use bullet points because the first time a potential customer looks at an advert, they don't read it. They scan it.

And when they scan an advert, the vast majority look at the following things:

Image, headline, bullet points and the 'PS' section at the bottom (if there is one)

When most people think about bullet points in advertising, they typically think of them as a list of features or benefits. As a decorator, you might currently use bullet points as a way of listing out the services you offer.

This is what most people do.

But there is a better way to use bullet points, and that is what we are going to cover here.

As an example, let's use the following bullet points that you'll typically see on an advert for a painter and decorator:

- 30 years' experience

- Dustless sanding
- Durable paints
- Spray finishing
- Fully insured
- Kitchen repainting specialists

These are bullet points in their most basic form. They simply list out the 'features'.

This is ok, but it's not good enough.

To make them better, I suggest you use the Jon Mears 'So, what?' test (patent pending).

Basically, whenever you write a bullet point you should then do your best impression of a grumpy old man and say 'So, what?'

As an example, let's use the bullet point '30 years' experience'

Now, in your grumpy old man voice....'So, what?'

Answer: Well, 30 years' experience means we have helped thousands of customers just like you to get exactly what they want from the decorating process. It also means we have proven to be trustworthy and reliable. Because if that wasn't the case we wouldn't still be in business.

Do you see how answering the question 'So, what?' makes you go one step further?

It helps you pull out the benefits to the customer.

This is far more appealing than simply listing out features and services.

Sometimes you can take it another step further. For example, let's look at the bullet 'Kitchen repainting specialists'.

Again, we ask the question… 'So, what?'

Answer: Well, we can repaint your kitchen at a fraction of the cost to replace it.

One more time…. 'So, what?'

Answer: Not only, does it mean you save money, but the process is much faster and far less hassle than you might think because we remove all the cupboards and spray them in our workshop. You could be showing off your newly transformed kitchen to friends in less than a week.

Do you see how we've gone one step deeper again? Now we have gone from a feature, to a benefit, to the *feeling* the customer will have.

This is what really drives customers to hire you. The feelings and emotions that you will create. The rise in status amongst their peers.

This is what we want to tap into.

To finish off, I'll use the original bullet points from the start of this chapter and enhance them with the 'So, what?' test, so you can see how you can bring benefits and feelings into your advertising.

- 30 years' experience – We've helped thousands of homeowners just like you to transform their homes into something beautiful. You can sit back and relax whilst our reliable and friendly staff turn your vision into a reality.
- Dustless sanding – We use the latest in dustless sanding technology to not just ensure a perfectly smooth finish, but also a clean working environment throughout the process. So, you don't have to hoover dust up every night!
- Durable paints – We work with manufacturers to test the latest in paint technology. Our durable paints mean that any scuffs or marks that might happen when we're gone can be easily cleaned and you won't need to touch it up with more paint! This saves you time and hassle.
- Spray finishing – We often use spray technology as part of our decorating process. This is not only much faster, meaning you get your space back sooner, but the finish is amazing. You'll have woodwork that looks as perfect as the paint job on a car.
- Fully insured – We have public liability insurance of £5,000,000. This means you can rest easy in the knowledge that if there were to be any issues or accidents, you are completely covered.
- Kitchen repainting specialists – Not only, does repainting your kitchen cost far less than

replacing, but the process is much faster and less hassle than you might think. We remove all the cupboards and spray them in our custom-built workshop. So, you'll have no concerns about overspray to clean up and you could be showing off your newly transformed kitchen to friends in less than a week.

SUMMARY

People tend to scan ads, so good bullet points are crucial to the success of your advert.

Use the 'So, what?' test to make sure your bullet points really tap into what the customer actually cares about.

Remember, nobody cares that you've been in business for 30 years. What they care about is that you have the experience and knowledge to be ready for every eventuality. They want to feel relaxed that you know what you're doing, and they have nothing to worry about.

Chapter 10. How to write the perfect sales document. Every time

Now we have the basics of creating great adverts. Here is an 8-step framework you can use and refer to whenever you are writing sales copy.

These 8 steps should be in every advert you write, whether it is a 20-page sales letter or a social media post.

1. **Headline + Sub-headline**
   Remember this is possibly the most important part of the entire thing.
2. **Define the problem you can solve**
   For example: Are you embarrassed of your kitchen? But don't want the expense or hassle of having it completely replaced?
3. **Explain how you can solve the issue**
   'We specialise in kitchen repainting. This is a more cost effective and quicker way to transform your kitchen.
4. **Bullet points**
   Add in bullet points using the techniques we discussed in chapter 9. Typically, 3-6 bullets will be most effective. But remember, it is about being concise rather than short. So, if you *need* more, don't be afraid to do it.

5. **Explain how you are qualified to solve this problem**
   Show before and after photos, add testimonials or explain the processes you use.
6. **Reduce the risk**
   Make the potential customer feel comfortable. Explain the process and show them that if they are not completely satisfied, they won't lose out. If you offer a guarantee on your work, mention it here.
7. **Call to action**
   Tell the customer in very clear and simple terms what they need to do next. 'Call now' 'Get quote' 'Learn more' 'Complete the below form'. You know the sort of thing I mean.
8. **PS / Summary**
   Remember, most people scan adverts in the first instance, and one of the things they read is the summary or 'PS' section. So, make sure you have one that sums up the whole offer nicely.

SUMMARY

It is always a good idea to use a structure when writing an advert. It means you will never forget anything important and maximise your chances of it being a success. This 8-step framework should help you answer all the questions a potential customer has before they are ready to start doing business with you. It has worked for me time and time again. Hopefully, it will bring you loads of success too.

Chapter 11. Advertising by Post

When you send an advert in the post (or 'mail' for any American readers) you have your work cut out.

It is said that people go through their post whilst stood over the waste bin.

I tend to agree with this.

So, whenever we create a leaflet, postcard, sales letter etc. we need to remember that we have only a fraction of a second to catch the attention of the customer and reel them in.

We also need to remember that our advert is also likely to be in a pile of other post. So, we need to work hard to stand out.

When people sit down to design a new leaflet or flyer, they often want it to look professional.

By doing this they accidentally tend to make it look the same as every other leaflet the customer gets.

What does this mean? It means it ends up in the bin with the rest of the 'junk mail'.

How do we avoid this?

Stop worrying so much about your advert looking 'professional' and simply focus on delivering your message in a simple and concise way.

Remember that what you write is far more important than what font you use. Or where you position the images, or how glossy the paper is.

So, don't stress on the 'creative' side of things.

Stick to the 8-point framework to deliver a brilliant sales message and you'll do well.

Important note: Whether you design the advert yourself, or whether you get someone else to do it. Always make sure your text is black on a white background.

Black text on a white background is the easiest to read and there are numerous studies that prove more people read adverts when they are written this way.

Reverse type such as white text on black, blue or any other coloured background makes it more difficult to read.

Yes, you might think it looks really fancy and beautiful, but fancy adverts don't pay the bills.

Your advert has one objective, and that is to create business. And the truth is that good quality content trumps beautiful designs every day of the week.

That said, there are a couple of 'design' features you can use to stand out and get more people to read your advert.

Non-Standard Sizing

Most leaflets that come through the door are A5 size. If you want to stand out, why not try A4? Or a business card? Or an A6 postcard.

If you go with postcard size, then why not print it on card? It'll be more expensive yes, but something like that is more likely to be kept by the customer. They might well stick it to the fridge. Especially if it has some sort of offer attached to it.

Lumpy Mail

Ever picked up a letter you weren't expecting and felt a lump in the envelope?

Strangely exciting isn't it?

What could it be?

Usually it is a pen, business card, sticker, voucher or even a fridge magnet.

Whatever it is, putting a 'lump' in your envelope massively increases the chances of your letter being opened.

So, although there is clearly a big expense to adding things like this to your campaign, it can easily pay for itself once all those extra enquiries come in.

Summary

The actual content of your leaflet is far more important than making it look beautiful and professional.

In fact, by not focusing too heavily on the creative side you are more likely to stand out and get your message read.

Always try to write with black text on a white (or cream) background. It massively increases the amount of people that read it. No amount of creative beauty can make up for this.

Try different sizes and textures to make people more likely to read and keep your adverts.

CHAPTER 12. BUSINESS CARDS

Yes, business cards are a form of advertising. Well, they are if you do it right.

You don't need me to tell you that there is not a lot of room on a business card. So, you must make sure every single word and image has a purpose.

The reason business cards are so powerful however, is because people treat them differently to most other adverts.

People tend not to throw away business cards.

They usually put them in their wallet or purse. Sometimes they will stick them to the fridge.

If they are very old school, they might even put them in a rolodex. If you are a younger reader and don't know what a rolodex is, give it a Google. It will blow your mind at how people used to store contact information before smartphones came around.

The temptation with a business card is to simply put your company logo, name, and contact information.

However, it can be so much more than this.

The trick is to remember that whenever you give someone a business card, they will likely store it away and not look at it again for months, even years.

This means that they will have probably forgotten who you are and what you do.

So, to combat this you need to make sure all this information is on your card.

If your company name doesn't explain what you do, then you need to make sure you have a line on the card that tells the customer this.

However, if you're company name is 'Grace's painting and decorating services' (or similar) you already this have this covered.

Because space is limited, it pays at this point if you have chosen a niche.

When we discussed this in chapter 2, I used an example of a social media post with 5 bullet points.

When you are designing a business card you only really have space for a few bullet points, usually on the back of the card, so you have two options.

1. List out all the services you offer. For example:

   - We spray uPVC windows and doors
   - Interior and exterior painting
   - Wallpaper hanging
   - Kitchen refurbishments
   - Commercial and residential work

2. Choose your niche and use the same amount of space to give the customer more information about what you do. For example:

   - We spray uPVC windows and doors
   - Using the latest spray equipment
   - Super durable paints so they look great all year round
   - Incredible care is taken during preparation to protect your home and ensure a perfect finish
   - Far more cost effective than replacing your windows

If you are still worried that limiting yourself to a particular niche is not right for your business, then don't panic.

Business cards are so cheap nowadays that you could just have two versions. One that talks about whatever you specialise in, and one that gives an overview of all the services you offer.

You can then simply decide which one to give to each particular customer depending on the situation.

SUMMARY

Business cards can be excellent advertising tools when used properly.

Don't be afraid to include bullet points about what you offer.

Design the busines card keeping in mind that by the time the customer reads it, they may well have forgotten who you are. So, you need it to be able to do a bit of selling for you. Otherwise the customer is unlikely to get in touch.

If you have a specialism, consider creating a separate business card just for that.

Chapter 13. Your website

Somewhere along the line people forgot that websites are a form of advertising.

In my opinion, the main point of a company website is to help generate sales.

However, for some reason, most people seem to focus on making their website pretty and fancy looking.

Whilst there is merit in a clean and professional looking website and if you can afford it, I would look to hire a professional to make sure it does look good.

I believe that the majority of your effort should *not* be focused on how it looks.

It should be focused on properly advertising your business and generating sales.

To do this effectively, you need to try and imagine what it is like for a potential customer visiting your website for the first time.

Your website needs to quickly answer any questions they may have so they can quickly, and confidently decide to get in touch with you.

Your website should be treated like any other sales document you create.

With this in mind, when you build the home page of your website, use the 8-step framework we covered in chapter 10.

Using this framework will mean that you quickly and concisely show visitors exactly why they should choose to work with you.

You'll answer any questions they might have; you'll show them pictures of your work and they will be able to see testimonials from people who have already used you.

Remember that everything you write should be in plain and simple language. Don't use technical terms to show off how clever you are.

Use the sort of language that you would if you were talking directly to the customer. Show some personality and make it easy to read.

When you are writing, the words should simply flow out of you. It should be easy. Because you're not trying too hard and you're not trying to think of long and complicated words that you'd never use in real life.

Finally, and I can't stress this enough, make it easy for people to get in touch with you!

You don't know exactly when the customer decides they want to call you.

It is impossible to know exactly which line of text, which bullet point or which photograph finally make the customer decide they are ready to contact you.

However, what you can do, is make sure that whenever they do make that decision, there is a big button saying, 'Contact us' or 'Get quote'.

I suggest that wherever the customer is on your website, they should always be able to see a button that takes them to your contact page.

You should have it at the top and bottom of every page on your website (in the header and footer).

There should be an option in the main menu for a 'Contact' page.

Don't be afraid to put these buttons halfway down the home page too.

The customer might decide after reading your bullet points that you are the right person for the job.

So put a 'Contact us' button there.

Don't make them scroll right to the top or bottom of the page just to find that information. They are ready now!

Summary

Yes, your website should look good. It should be a good representation of you, your brand and your values.

However, do not lose sight of the fact that your website has a purpose.

And that purpose is to make you money.

Your website is a big advert for your business. It should be a place where potential customers can find out everything they need to know about what you do, how you do it and why you are the best.

Pretty websites don't pay the bills. Websites that effectively sell your services do.

Don't forget this.

Chapter 14. Case studies

A great case study can be an amazing advert for your business. For the purposes of this chapter I'm going to talk about written case studies.

You can of course use video, but I am dedicating a chapter to video advertising later in the book.

Properly done, a case study can be an amazing advert for your business.

I would recommend you have at least 1 case study on your website, but 2 or 3 would be even better.

When a potential customer reads one of your case studies, it should help them understand exactly what it'll be like if they hire you.

It should answer any niggling little questions they might have, and it should give them confidence that you are the right person for the job.

Structuring the case study

Whenever I write a case study, I like to use following format.

1. Start with who the customer is and where abouts they live. (People will find it easier to relate to if the example you use is somewhere

near to them). Introduce the problem or explain why the customer got in touch with you.
2. Explain the solution you proposed and why the customer chose you.
3. Show the processes you used and explain why you did it that way. Include information such as how long it took, what colours the customer went with and what equipment you needed. Talk about how all of this benefitted the customer with the end result.
4. Detail any unexpected problems you ran into and how you resolved them.
5. End with a quote or testimonial from the happy customer and your company logo and contact information.

To give you a better idea of how to do this, let's use this structure to write an example case study.

For the purposes of the example, let's pretend we are repainting a front door.

CASE STUDY – MRS. JONES, OXFORD

In a small village just outside Oxford you'll find the beautiful country home of Mrs. Jones.

After several years of the Great British weather taking its toll on exterior of her home, she knew that her front door either needed to be repaired or replaced.

When Mrs. Jones contacted us, she was unsure about what was the best thing to do, so we arranged to visit her later that week to have a look at the situation and see if we could come up with a suitable solution.

After speaking with Mrs. Jones, it was clear that making sure her home kept its traditional look was very important. So, after carefully inspecting the door we decided that repairing the existing timber door would be the best thing to do.

After putting together a quotation for Mrs. Jones and giving her time to discuss the it with the rest of her family she decided to go ahead with the work, and we arranged to start 6 weeks later (weather dependent).

To make sure the exterior of the door would not just look great but also stay protected from the weather, good preparation was key.

We started by sanding back all the flaking paint to make sure we had a sound base to start on. We used our dustless sanding equipment to make sure no dust got all over Mrs. Jones' flowers!

When sanding the flaking paint back, we found there was quite a bit of damage to the door. Water had got in and caused large areas of the door to go soft and rotten.

To solve this problem, we then cut out all the rotten wood from the door and repaired it using an exterior grade wood filler, which we have personally tested and know to be extremely durable.

A primer coat was then applied to help increase adhesion and to create another barrier of protection for the door.

Any final small blemishes were then filled and sanded back before the first topcoat of paint was applied.

We used a trade only exterior paint to ensure maximum protection and had it mixed to Mrs. Jones choice of colour - Hague blue.

After the first topcoat we gently sanded the door once more with a very fine sandpaper. This means that the final coat goes on extra smooth, giving the door a 'factory new' finish.

As a little finishing touch, we also cleaned up the brass handle and knocker, so they looked brand new again.

The job took 3 days in total and Mrs. Jones was delighted with the finish, not to mention the fact that our work comes with a 2-year guarantee.

Mrs. Jones commented 'Grace and the team at HGA decorators were an absolute pleasure to have working at our home. They were polite and considerate throughout the process and we are over the moon with the results. We've already booked them in to do the window frames later in the year'

We'd like to say thanks to Mrs. Jones for being such a great customer…and thanks for all the lovely cake!

Final tips

Remember to take loads of photographs throughout the process and of course make sure the customer is happy for you to use them on your website.

Scatter the images throughout the article to help the customer visualise the process as they read.

A case study doesn't need to be long. 1 page of A4 is usually enough.

Summary

Use case studies to help potential customers see exactly what working with you will be like and to educate them on the expertise you bring to different situations.

Make sure you follow a structure so that you don't forget anything.

Make it easy to read and use plenty of photographs.

Consider having 2 or 3 case studies on your website to show case the different types of work you offer.

Chapter 15. Email marketing

Joe Girard was an American salesman who held the honour of officially being the World's greatest salesman – According to the Guinness book of records.

Girard sold 13,001 cars at a Chevrolet dealership between 1963 and 1978 and was recognised by the Guinness Book of World Records as the seller of the most cars in a year (1,425 in 1973).

How did he do this?

Well, Girard was doing something nobody else was at the time.

If you ever bought a car from Girard, you would then go on to receive a handwritten greetings card from him every month.

That's right. Every year he would have 12 cards designed and would send them out to all his customers every single month.

By the end of his career it was said he was employing a team of people to help do it. Afterall, he was sending over 10,000 cards a month.

This simple act was enough to generate so much repeat business and so many referrals that Girard earned a small fortune as a car salesman.

So, what was the magical content he put on the cards each month?

It was simple. Each card simply said:

'I like you'

That was it. No fancy marketing messages. No special offers. Just the single line 'I like you'

Now, at this point you might be thinking, that's a lovely story, but what has it got to do with email marketing?

I mean, he wasn't using email.

Email wasn't even in use back then.

Well, if you ask me, this story perfectly explains the power of keeping in touch with your customers.

And now we have email, you can do it a whole lot cheaper and easier than Girard did.

Girard proves that by simply staying top of mind, your customers are far more likely to recommend you and give you repeat business.

In the rest of this chapter, I will explain how to set up and use email marketing to grow your business. Starting with…

SETTING UP FOR EMAIL MARKETING

Getting ready for email marketing has never been simpler. In fact, you can be up and running in a matter of minutes.

To start, search the internet for 'Email marketing' providers. There are plenty available.

Personally, I use 'MailChimp.com' and I would happily recommend it to you.

At time of writing, MailChimp is a free service for anyone who has fewer than 2,000 subscribers to their email list. So, it is a great place to start.

Simply go to the website, register your details and you are ready. It takes literally minutes.

BUILDING YOUR LIST OF CONTACTS

The next stage is to start getting people on to your email marketing list.

Firstly, you might already have a file with the email addresses of all your previous customers. So, assuming your local or national data protection laws allow you to, then I would add these into your database straight away.

NB: You could always send an initial email to these customers explaining what you are doing and allow them to unsubscribe straight away if they want to.

Next, you should follow the steps on MailChimp to add an option to your website for people to join your mailing list. You've seen these before. It'll be something simple like 'Enter your email here to join my mailing list'

I have this at the bottom of every page on my website if you wanted to have a look www.jmears.co.uk (Feel free to join my mailing list).

You now have the basics in place.

Potential customers who visit your website can join your list, and you can keep adding every new customer you work for (assuming you get their permission).

And don't worry about having to 'manage' the list. MailChimp does all that for you. At the bottom of every email you send via MailChimp, there will automatically be an 'Unsubscribe' option.

If anyone ever clicks the unsubscribe button MailChimp automatically remove them from your list. You don't have to do anything.

There is one more thing you can do to increase the size of your list though. Something that if done correctly could mean you have more subscribers than you know what to do with. In the marketing world we call these secret weapons…

LEAD MAGNETS

What the hell is a lead magnet I hear you ask?

A lead magnet is something we use to get more people to join our mailing list.

Normally this will be an offer of something free or very cheap that is of interest to your target customer.

For example, a lead magnet that has been very successful for me on my own website is something I called:

'My 5 favourite social media tips for decorators'

Nothing complicated here. It is simply a short article that details my 5 favourite social media tips, that I think are useful for decorators.

How it works is that whenever someone subscribes to my email list, MailChimp automatically sends an email that I've written that includes the 5 tips.

Take the time to think about a lead magnet for your business.

Think about what knowledge you have as a decorator, that you could give away for free and is of value to potential customers.

For example, if your target customers are homeowners and you specialise in exterior masonry work you could create something like:

'5 signs your exterior walls need attention'

In this document you could talk about how if a property has signs of mould, cracks or blown render then it needs to be looked at.

You could show people how to identify these things, what problems they might cause and how to prevent them from getting worse.

Information like this is potentially very valuable to your customers as they will know that prevention is often cheaper than cure.

When you are creating a lead magnet it is best to think of 2 or 3 and test each of them out separately. You might find that some perform far better than others.

Now you have a lead magnet written up, all you need to do is add it to an automated 'Welcome email' on the MailChimp website. Again, this can be set up quickly and easily. Literally a couple of minutes.

This single piece of work will help you grow your email subscriber list much faster.

Think about it. Without it, you are simply saying 'Join my mailing list' …and well, that is not very appealing to most people.

But now you are saying, 'Here, have this really useful piece of information. All I want in return is your email address, so that I can send it to you'.

People simply enter their email and MailChimp send the information automatically. And at the same time, MailChimp adds them to your list.

You will literally be doing it in your sleep.

SENDING EMAILS

We now have our email campaign software (MailChimp) set up and we are starting to grow our list of subscribers automatically.

All we must do now is start sending emails.

There are a couple of ways you can do this. You can send emails as and when you have some useful information for people or when you have a great offer to share.

You can send simple monthly emails like our friend Joe Girard did.

Or you can do both.

Which is what I suggest you do.

Job number one: plan out the simple messages for the year.

This can be as easy as theming the email to the relevant month and essentially just saying hello.

For example, January would be 'Happy new year', February 'Happy Valentines', October 'Happy Halloween' and so on.

This is literally 20 minutes of planning and it'll sort you out for the whole year.

I can almost guarantee that doing this alone will bring in some business for you.

But, if you want to take it up a level, before you send each monthly email, take an hour to yourself and think about whether there is some extra value you can offer.

Maybe every now and then you send out an article like your lead magnet.

Towards the end of the year you could send some info on the predicted colour trends for the next year.

In January or February, you could do a quick article on how to tell if your timber windows are rotting and need attention. Then put a simple line at the bottom of the email saying that you are now taking bookings for exterior work in the Spring.

You could also use the emails to give news about your business. Perhaps you have been on a training course and got a new qualification, which means you are now offering a new service of uPVC spraying.

There are loads of options and once you get going, you'll be surprised how easy it is to do these things.

But even if you decide you can't be bothered with writing articles every month then it doesn't matter.

Joe Girard became the world's greatest salesman by sending a note that simply said, 'I like you'.

And if this simple practice can do that for him, then you can be sure that a quick email each month can help your business massively.

SUMMARY

Email marketing doesn't need to be complicated or time consuming. Get set up with an online email marketing platform (for free) and start keeping in touch with your customers. The results could blow you away.

Chapter 16. Social media advertising

In this chapter I am only going to talk about paid advertising on social media.

If you want to learn about how to use social media to grow your business without paid ads you can check out my first book 'Sales & Marketing for Decorators' where there are several chapters dedicated to it. Or you can visit my website www.jmears.co.uk/social-media-for-decorators/ where you can find several free blogs all about how to do it.

So, paid advertising on social media.

Most people have tried it. Most people have failed at it.

If you are someone who has failed to make social media advertising work for your business in the past, then don't worry.

It happens to everyone. Myself included.

In fact, most of my adverts 'fail' on social media.

This is the beauty of paid advertising on social media. You can fail quick and often. Without spending a fortune. And this is exactly what you should be doing.

This probably sounds like a very strange thing to say; however, you need to realise that the vast majority of adverts created actually fail.

As brilliant as you think your advert might be, you never know if it is any good until you start using it.

You'll never create the perfect advert straight off the bat.

An advert that performs well is an advert that has been continually tested and tweaked until it starts working.

So, the ability to fail quickly and without wasting much money is a huge advantage.

I'll give you an example.

Recently I ran an advertising campaign on Facebook for my first book.

To start, I created 6 versions of the advert.

Remember the split testing or A/B testing we talked about in Chapter 5? Well, that's what I was doing.

I tried the same headline and text with 6 different visuals (Videos / photos).

I then started by spending just £2 per day in total for these 6 adverts.

The purpose of my advert was to get people to click on the advert and buy my book from Amazon.

I would measure the results in 'Cost per click' (CPC).

For anyone not familiar, CPC is how much money you need to spend on the advert to get someone to click on it.

For example, if you were spending £2 per day on an advert and you got 1 click per day, your CPC would be £2.

However, if you got 2 clicks per day your CPC would be £1.

4 clicks per day = £0.50 CPC.

This is something Facebook gives you real time information on. You don't have to wait until the end of each day.

After 4 days I found 1 video and 1 image that outperformed all the others.

The video was averaging £0.38 per click and the image £0.40 per click (all the others were nearly double the cost per click).

This was a great start, after just 4 days and having spent only £8 I had 2 adverts that were performing twice as well as the others I created.

Imagine if I'd have only created 1 advert and it was one of the poorer performing ads. If I scaled up my spend on that ad, I could have wasted huge amounts of money.

So, what did I do next?

Well, I duplicated the 2 best performing adverts so that I had 4 running, but on the 2 new ones I made a change to the headline.

After doing this I found that one of the new headlines was performing brilliantly, it had brought my cost per click down to under £0.20.

I repeated this process once more and managed to bring the cost per click down to £0.15.

Now that I had a well optimised ad, I cut two of them and focused on one video ad and one photograph ad. Both with the same headline.

Both of them were giving me results of around £0.15 per click.

I then changed my daily spend to £1.50 on each (£3 per day total).

This meant that as long as I sold just 1 book per day, I would make enough profit to cover the cost of the ads and a little bit for myself.

These 2 adverts went on to generate more than 5x the number of clicks and doubled my daily sales (compared to the original 6 adverts).

What can we learn from this?

Well, firstly, I created 10 adverts in total. 8 of which failed. So, we learn that it is normal for the majority of your ads to fail. It is just part of the process.

Secondly, we learned that social media ads are brilliant for getting quick and cheap feedback on whether your ads are any good.

In the example, I used Facebook, but you will find the same situation with most social media platforms.

Paid advertising on social media is crucial for you to learn what works and what doesn't. It helps you to understand that advertising is something you need to continually work at. Something you need to constantly test and tweak.

Paid advertising gives you real time feedback on the performance of your adverts. This is something that you just don't get when you post adverts for free.

Now, the purpose of this example was to teach you that the true test of an advert is to put it in front of your audience, see if it works and if or when it doesn't, then you need to tweak it and try again.

However, it makes sense to give ourselves the best chances right from the off so that you can shortcut your way to a great performing ad.

Here are some tips I've found to be really effective when creating social media adverts.

SOCIAL MEDIA TOP TIPS

1. Videos will outperform images in the vast majority of cases. I've personally found they usually have a CPC that is twice as good as a comparable image. If you have the choice of using a video or a photo, I would always go with a video.
2. Use emojis in your text. Don't overdo it, but one or two emojis always seem to help my ads. They break up the text and make it more readable, they catch people's attention, and they make it look like less of a 'traditional' advert. Meaning people are less likely to scroll straight past.
3. Use the 8-step framework from Chapter 10 to make sure the sales copy you use in the advert is as good as it can be.
4. Remember headlines are incredibly important. Spend a lot of time on them!
5. Show your adverts to trusted friends and family first. Remember you're not looking for them to say they like the ad. You want them to say they would do what the ad is asking. I.E. they would click for more info, give you a call, hire you etc. NB: When I show an advert to someone about my book I don't care if they like the style of it. All I want is for them to say 'Woah, that book sounds brilliant. That would help me. Can I buy a copy?'

If they say anything else, then the advert is not doing its job properly.
6. Proofread your adverts. Don't let yourself down with sloppy spelling and grammar. If you are not very good at this then ask a friend or family member to help.
7. Tailor your ads to the social media network you are posting it on. It needs to feel right and fit the culture of the platform. Remember, an advert that works well on Instagram probably wouldn't work as well on LinkedIn.
8. Write adverts as if you are talking directly to one person. This is a good rule for all advertising, but it is particularly useful on social media. Remember that scrolling through social media on your phone is a very personal thing. Everything on your feed has been designed for you. It is all your friends and the things you enjoy most. Make sure your advert is the same.

Summary

Paid advertising on social media is about failing often and failing cheaply. Test, tweak and test again.

You'll never create a brilliant advert first time. You need to get used to that fact. Don't get disheartened and certainly don't give up.

Use the tips from this chapter to improve your chances of creating a great advert and then get out there and start testing.

The lessons you learn from creating and testing social media adverts can help you in every form of advertising.

I'd recommend spending at least a small amount of money on it every month.

Chapter 17. Advertising in Print

Whether it is a national newspaper or a local parish magazine, most decorators will at some point want to try advertising in print.

There are a couple of challenges when it comes to creating adverts for print.

Firstly, you usually get charged by the word, or by the size of the ad. Either way, keeping it concise is important.

Secondly, print adverts have been around for a long time. Which means it is difficult to be original.

The first thing you need to decide when creating an advert for print, is the size. Are you going for a small box in the classified section? Quarter page? Double page spread?

The first thing I can tell you is that double page spreads barely tend to outperform single page adverts.

So, even if you are swimming in money, there isn't much point to these.

After that, you simply need to test what works best for you.

As with social media advertising, you need to decide the objective of your print ad and work out a way to measure it.

I would say the best way to measure the advert is to work out how much profit it generates for you. As a painter and decorator, you could measure this by simply asking every customer how they heard about you and recording how much money you make from each customer who came from the print ad.

If you are running adverts in several magazines and newspapers, then you might want to consider using a promo code that the customer must quote when making an enquiry. This will make it easier to track how each advert is performing.

The reason I think it is best to measure the performance of print ads based on the profits they bring you is that is the best way to measure your return on investment (ROI).

ROI is important in all advertising but particularly so in print ads. The reason I say this is that the difference in pricing for print advertising can be insane. Full page ads in some magazines can cost you a small fortune, and you might find similar results using a cheaper classified ad.

Also, print advertising seems to work differently to most other advertising. Often you won't get immediate and measurable results like you do with things such as social media.

For example, if you put an advert in the local parish magazine it might perform poorly for the first 6 months and then start to pick up. People say this is because when you advertise in local magazines like this it takes a while for people to become familiar with you and trust you.

You might also find that half page or full-page ads in larger publications stop performing after a period of time because people start to get used to seeing it and subconsciously start skipping past it. So, you have to spend time redesigning it every few months, otherwise your ROI gets worse and worse.

Whereas small and cheap classified ads can run at a profitable ROI for months and sometime years.

Now we know how to measure the performance of your ads, let's talk about how to create and design them effectively.

For the purposes of this chapter I'm going to talk about full/half page ads and classified ads. I group full- and half-page ads together because I think you can achieve much the same results with them and I would design them in a similar way.

I'll discuss classified ads because I think they are most popular with painters and decorators and often give the best ROI.

FULL AND HALF PAGE ADS

It is easy to over think the design of a print ad, so I'm going to give you a basic layout that will cover pretty much everything you need, and to be honest the content of your ad is way more important than what it looks like, so don't stress yourself out.

From top to bottom of the page this is an effective way to layout an advert:

Visual (Photo / sketch / diagram)

Headline

Sub headline

Opening paragraphs

Bullet points

Closing paragraphs

Call to action

PS

The only thing that will change from full page to half page is the size of the visual and the amount of text and bullet points you use. The layout should stay basically the same.

One quick point before I go through each of these sections. Remember the golden rule of copywriting I mentioned earlier. Always have your text as black on white background. Don't use reverse type as it is harder to read and will automatically reduce the amount of people who look at your ad. You are literally just throwing money away. Pretty adverts are useless if nobody reads them.

Also, don't use extra small font sizes to cram in more information. Again, it'll make it too hard to read and people will skip right on by.

VISUAL

The job of the visual is to get people's attention and to intrigue them enough to start reading your advert.

We covered images in chapter 8, so you should already have a good idea of what sort of images you should use in advertising.

To make it even more simple, I'm going to tell you to use a 'before and after' shot.

As a decorator, you'll have loads of these, and they are absolutely fantastic for what you are trying to achieve here. Just make sure your visual matches what you are talking about in the advert. For example, if your advert is about uPVC window spraying, don't have a before and after picture of a recent kitchen you painted. Obviously.

Also, make sure the images are relatable for the audience. If you are advertising in a local paper where the average house price is £200k. Don't put a before and after shot of a £10m mansion you just worked on. And vice versa.

Pro tip: Make sure you caption your images. When people scan through adverts, they typically stop to read the captions on images. So, this is a great place to put a quick sales message.

HEADLINE

There is a bit of debate about whether the headline should be above or below the visual. In my opinion, the fact there is a debate about it means that it probably doesn't make much of a difference. Personally, I've never seen a difference in results. That said, my current preference is to have the headline underneath the visual.

We've already had a full chapter on headlines so don't worry, I'm not going to go on about them again.

I will just remind you that they are incredibly important, you should spend a lot of time creating them and make sure that your headline relates to the visual in your ad.

SUB HEADLINE

You don't *need* a sub headline, but they often help. For me, sub headlines are simply an extension of the main headline.

As you know, you need to keep the main headline brief and make sure it creates some curiosity in the reader.

The job of the sub headline is to continue this and bridge the gap from the headline to the main text.

Here is an example:

Visual: Before and after photo of a kitchen that has been repainted.

Headline: How the Jones' saved £4,964 on their new kitchen.

Sub headline: Discover how our latest decorating service is saving homeowners thousands AND increasing the value of their home.

See how it works? The sub headline gives you a bit more information and helps make you curious enough to read the main block of text that follows.

OPENING PARAGRAPHS

The job of the opening paragraphs is to capture the interest of the reader and pull them in. Make them short and snappy. Avoid long sentences and try to keep each paragraph to a maximum of 3 to 4 lines. Anymore and it is too much work for most people. They are not invested enough to make the effort to read long and difficult block of text yet. Remember to also start covering points from the 8-step framework we discussed in chapter 10.

Bullet Points

We covered how to write amazing bullet points in chapter 9. So, I won't go over that again here.

The reason they are important for a good advert is that firstly, they help you get your point across concisely.

And secondly, when someone scans an advert (which most people do the first-time round) one of the things they will read is the bullet points. So, make sure you have some!

Closing Paragraphs

By this point in the ad, you are looking to solve the problem your customer has and start leading into how they should get in touch with you.

Call to Action

Nice and simple this bit. Make sure at the bottom of your ad you make it very clear what the customer should do next. Whether that is call you, visit your website, cut out a coupon or even send you a text.

Whatever it is, make it very simple and very clear.

PS

The other thing people read when they scan through an advert is the PS section. So again, you need to make sure you have one.

The PS section only needs to be a couple of lines long. Use it to sum up the problem and offer you are making and remind them how to get in touch.

If we continue with the kitchen example it might look something like this:

PS: We offer free quotations and can usually meet you in under 48 hours.

So, if you are ready transform your kitchen WITHOUT the massive price tag of replacing it.

Get in touch with Harriet on 0121…

CLASSIFIED ADS

A staple of the painter and decorator's advertising strategy for decades is the humble classified ad.

You don't have much space with these ads, so they all tend to look like this:

Alexander's decorators

All aspects of interior and exterior decorating

Call 0121… for a FREE quote

Ok, so this sort of advert does a job, and it will get you some business.

But it could be better.

For the sake of this section, let's say the average classified ad allows you to have 20 words + a phone number.

At this point, it really pays off to have a niche. As you can dedicate every word to one topic.

For example, instead of saying something generic like:

We cover all aspects of interior and exterior decorating in the Oxford area. No job too big or small. Call 0121... (20 words + a phone number)

You could instead really sell the benefits of why someone should choose you. Example:

We paint kitchens to a 'factory new' finish for a fraction of the cost to replace. In any colour! Call 0121... (20 words + a phone number)

It also pays at this point if your company name incorporates what you do. This will save you words in the text. So, if you are just starting your company, consider naming your company accordingly. *Grace's Hand Painted Kitchens*...or *Alexander Painter & Decorator.*

The best advice I can give you for classified ads however is to try and make them different.

To do this you might have to sit down one day and try to write 10 or 20 different versions. But it will be worth it.

Think about it. In every local paper or magazine, you'll find half a dozen ads for painters and decorators. If your advert looks the same as all the others, then a potential customer has no reason to call you over anyone else.

Sure, you'll get your fair share of calls.

But if you want to get more than your fair share, then you need to do something different. Whether that is specialising in a particular area or just using a different style of language to everyone else.

Also, remember there is nothing to stop you running multiple classified ads. So, you could do an ad that is for general painting and decorating services and then a separate one for your specialist service. If you are unsure of what to do then I would try this. Then measure the results of each advert and see what is bringing in the best business.

SUMMARY

Print ads can be a great source of business. Remember that testing and tweaking adverts is key to maximising your return on investment (ROI). Follow the templates I have set out and you are well on your way.

Remember, pretty adverts are useless if nobody reads them. So, focus on the content of your advert and don't stress yourself out with the design of it.

PS: The tips for classified ads could also be used for online versions and lead websites. Such as e-zines and Checkatrade etc.

Chapter 18. Blogs

Writing blogs has several benefits for you and your business.

1. Blogs keep your website fresh and loaded with keywords. This means you'll rank higher on Google searches and get more customer enquiries
2. They are a great way to educate your customers and build a reputation for being the specialist in your field
3. When written properly, they will help customers get to know you and your business. Building familiarity like this will help build trust and lead to more work
4. Creating blogs is great writing practice. Which is a skill that will benefit you in so many ways. It'll mean you get better at writing compelling adverts, better at writing emails that help you get what you want, proposals that make the customer want to buy and loads more.
5. Writing blogs can also be a gateway to opportunities you won't even imagine.

Let's go through each of these points to explain why writing a blog is a great way of advertising for decorators.

Rank higher on Google

We all know that one of the first things a potential customer does when looking to hire a decorator is to have a look on Google.

This means that making sure you are high up in the search rankings is crucial to your success. As a minimum you need to be on the first page for key search terms like 'Painter and decorator near me'

Google uses an incredibly complicated algorithm to make sure the most relevant websites are listed at the top of any given search.

This algorithm is also constantly being updated and improved, so I can't go into detail about every little thing that works today. As it might not be as effective tomorrow.

Two things that have always remained true though, is Google love websites that:

1. Are regularly updated
2. Have lots of keywords related to the search topic

For these two reasons, blogs are a great way to keep towards the top of the rankings, without spending any money.

Educate your customers

A complaint I hear from decorators on an almost daily basis is that customers don't understand the skill and time involved in creating the perfect finish. And because of this, customers don't value the service a good decorator is providing.

This of course means that customers don't want to pay what a decorator is really worth.

A great way to help solve this problem is to start educating customers on the processes and skills involved in good decorating.

This is something that you could do by simply creating some regular blogs talking about your day to day processes as a professional painter and decorator.

The more you educate your customers on the skills you bring to a job, the more they will value you and the more they will then be prepared to pay. Simple.

BUILDING FAMILIARITY

When you write, you should do it with your own personal style. Good writing should make the reader feel like they are having a conversation with you.

I hope that the way I write makes you feel like you know me.

My writing should give you a good idea of my general values and views on the world. Even my sense of humour.

If you write regular blogs your readers will get to know you too.

The familiarity they will feel for you then leads them to trust you and be more comfortable hiring you.

Remember that a lot of people are worried about having a tradesperson in their home because they are essentially a stranger.

If you can make a potential customer feel just a little bit more comfortable with you than your competition, then you are more likely to win the job.

WRITING PRACTICE

As you've learned throughout this book, being able to write clear and convincing copy is a massive advantage in business.

The better you are at writing the more business you'll get.

Better writing means better performing adverts. It means emails that get more responses. And proposals that close more deals.

Unfortunately, once we leave school we tend to stop writing on a regular basis. This means we get rusty and lose our edge.

Writing blogs will help clear out the cobwebs and give you a massive advantage over your competitors.

Even if you're too shy to post them on your website or social media, I would still recommend you try writing them on a regular basis. You'll be surprised just how quickly you improve and how much of a benefit it brings to your business.

Gateway to other opportunities

Writing a blog can lead to opportunities you won't even think of.

For example, I started writing a blog and within a year I'd been offered to speak at industry events, I wrote a book, I even appeared on podcasts and radio shows. It is crazy. There are loads of things like this that could happen for you. Who knows, you could get offered a radio slot, you might appear on a TV show or get asked to do a particularly prestigious job because you are known as an industry expert. The point is, you don't know until you start doing it.

How to write a blog

Now we know *why* you should write a blog, let me give you some quick tips on *how* to do it:

Choose a topic

Firstly, pick a topic that you think might be of interest to your potential customers.

For example:

- How to paint furniture like a pro
- Why re-painting your kitchen could save you thousands
- How to paint your masonry and add thousands to the value of your home

Start with something your potential customer might want to know and then use the blog to explain everything about it.

Remember, you want to use the blog as a bit of a sales piece too.

So, if you're writing about repainting a kitchen, don't be afraid to talk about all the processes and equipment involved. Explain why spraying the cabinets gives a better finish and how knowing the best paints on the market means a more durable finish.

By the end of the blog the customer should know how to do it themselves. But they should also know it is better to leave it to a professional like you.

LENGTH

The length of the blog is not that important if you ask me. Some people will say 1,000 to 1,500 words is best. Personally, I'd just use the rule that it needs to be as long as it needs to be.

If you can get your point across in 500 words, then fine.

If you write 3,000 words, but it is as concise as you can make it, then that's fine too.

First Draft

When writing out your first draft, just let it flow. Don't edit as you go along. Simply type as the words come to you. Even if it doesn't make much sense.

The first draft is about getting all your ideas down.

Second Draft

Once you've written your first draft, walk away and do something else for at least an hour. Preferably leave it overnight.

You need to create some distance between you and your writing.

The reason for this is that the next time you look at that first draft you need to read it like it is someone else's work.

This will make it easier for you to create the second draft.

Things to do in the second draft are: Cut out any sections that you don't need. Essentially, if it doesn't add anything to the blog, then remove it. Next, you need to tidy up any sentences that don't make much sense and finally, add any bits in you think will enhance your message.

PROOFREAD

The last thing to do is proofread. Check all spelling, punctuation, and grammar. If you are not very good at this then use the inbuilt software on Microsoft word to tidy it up. There are also great apps you can download, like Grammarly.

Failing that, ask someone else to look at it.

Often it is difficult to spot your own mistakes, so if you have someone who can run their eye over it, then I would definitely recommend it.

SUMMARY

Writing blogs is more than just a good way to improve your ranking on Google.

They can help you to gain the trust of potential customers, set yourself apart from the competition and even help you write better and more convincing adverts. All of which means increased profits for you and your business.

Chapter 19. Video

Like it or not, using video in your advertising is something you really need to do.

In my experience, video adverts outperform images 4 out of 5 times.

There are a few reasons I can think of for this.

Video ads stand out and catch your attention. Particularly when scrolling through social media.

People are lazy and would rather watch a short video than read a few paragraphs.

And it is often quicker and easier to explain things using a video. Rather than a single image and text.

Before we go any further, let's address the elephant in the room.

Creating videos is more difficult that other types of advertising. You must shoot multiple angles; you ideally need to be able to do basic editing and let's not forget the biggest problem…most people are camera shy.

Fortunately, the technical side of things is becoming far easier nowadays. In fact, you can do most basic functions on your smart phone. I often do.

This includes trimming and stitching multiple images and videos together, adding music, and even adding basic text overlays and graphics.

And with every update there is on your smartphone and social media, this is getting easier and easier.

If you are worried about the technical aspect of things. Spend half an hour watching some YouTube tutorials and I promise you'll pick up the basics really quickly.

The bigger problem, however, is camera shyness.

There are two things I can tell you to combat this.

1. Even if you don't want to appear in front of camera, there are still plenty of ways to use video to advertise
2. People don't care nearly as much as you think when you appear on camera. Yes, you will be super critical of yourself and pick holes in everything you say and do, but the truth is, not only do people not really care, but also, when you first start doing videos, hardly anyone will be watching anyway. So, my advice is just to suck it up and give it a go. By the time loads of people are watching your videos you'll have loads of practice under your belt and you'll be looking natural and easy in front of camera.

Video is a massive topic and honestly it could be a book on its own, but for this chapter I am going to focus on 4 types of video that are simple to produce and can be really effective for attracting new customers.

Slideshows

The first type of video is probably the easiest and the one you'll feel most comfortable using. A simple slideshow.

As I've already mentioned, one of the most powerful things in the advertising world is the before and after picture.

And as a painter and decorator you will have loads of these.

So, for your first video advert, all you need to do is get together all your favourite before and after photos, a picture of your company logo and an image with your contact information on it.

Now, using your smartphone you can select all these images and put them into a slideshow. There is a one-click option to create a slideshow on most phones. If you still struggle with this then either look for a YouTube video to show you how to do it or ask a more tech savvy friend or family member. It'll literally take them 30 seconds.

PS: See what I mean about videos often being an easier way to explain things? I've already recommended you go to YouTube twice in this chapter alone.

A good slideshow video is a no brainer for me. It is quick to make and quick to update with new photos.

Simply start with a title slide of your company name and logo, do half a dozen before and after photos and close with your contact information. Easy.

A slideshow video like this can be used on social media and on your website or Facebook business page. It not only shows potential customers how great you are at your job, but it will also give them inspiration on colours and design ideas. Meaning you don't lose time further down the road when they can't quite decide what shade of white they want in the downstairs cupboard.

It is a great way to advertise and will almost certainly lead to more business.

Behind the scenes videos

I love 'behind the scenes vides', not only are they good at catching the interest of potential customers, but also the more 'rough and ready' the video, the better it tends to perform.

This is perfect for anyone just starting to use video as part of their advertising strategy. As essentially you don't want it to be too clean and slick.

You want it to be a slightly lower quality as it feels more natural.

There are two things I think you should use 'behind the scenes' videos for.

1. To build familiarity with you and your company
2. To educate potential customers on the skills and techniques you use to do your job so well

BUILDING FAMILIARITY

We've spoken about the value of this in previous chapters, so you'll know that it is a great way to build trust and put you ahead of the competition.

Try making some short videos when you are working on a job. You don't have to be on camera, you can just narrate over the top.

Homeowners are often worried about having tradesmen in their house so why not show them with a couple of short videos how you work?

You could show them how you use top quality floor protection and dustsheets to make sure all the customer's possessions don't get paint or dust on them.

You could do a 10 second video explaining how your current customer works from home, so you are being extra careful not to be noisy and that you've arranged a schedule for any loud works such as using your electric sander.

The videos don't need to be long. Just short and simple little videos that will help potential customers get to know you, like you and trust you.

EDUCATING THE CUSTOMER

Trying to explain to a customer who knows nothing about decorating exactly what you're doing and why it takes the time it does can be tricky. So why not show them?

A quick video showing how you've had to do so much filling it would almost have been quicker to replaster it. Or a video of you rubbing down between coats of paint to get the perfect finish could prove very valuable in your social media advertising.

Things like this will help educate the customer on the processes used by a good decorator. This will then mean people value you and your work more. Which not only leads to more customers, but also better-quality customers.

CASE STUDY OR TESTIMONIAL VIDEOS

In chapter 14 I gave you a structure to write a case study. The good news is that this structure also works for video. The better news is that video case studies are even more powerful.

When you are creating a video case study you need a couple of things.

First, you need to take lots of photos and short videos of the work. Make sure you have something that shows what it was like before you started, something to show each stage of the process and then what it looked like when you finished.

The second thing you need is a video of the customer giving you a testimonial.

This can be tricky because some people are camera shy. But you just need to ask everyone you work for and eventually you will get someone willing to help you out.

It is worth it though. So, make sure you get it done.

When you can show a potential customer a video testimonial from someone just like them, it will give them confidence in you like nothing else.

And don't think it needs to be a long and detailed testimonial. 5-10 seconds is more than enough.

Once you have all the ingredients. Simply stitch all the photos and video clips together like you did for the slideshow video.

TALKING TO THE CAMERA VIDEOS

The fourth and final type of video I'd recommend is you talking directly to the camera.

Yes, it is scary and yes, it is difficult, but talking directly to the camera can produce results unlike any other.

You can use this type of video for several things. Firstly, it is another great way to educate the customer on things. Secondly, it is brilliant for building familiarity and trust.

But thirdly, and perhaps most important it is a great way to sell your services and advertise your business.

To put it into perspective, 9 of the 10 most successful adverts I've ever put together were me talking directly to the camera.

So how do you do it?

Well, here are 5 tips I use on all my videos.

1. **Write a script**. If you plan on saying any more than a couple of sentences, then you should write a script. Believe me, for some reason as soon as you start talking to a camera your mind can go blank. Even introducing yourself can seem difficult. To combat this, write a script with exactly what you want to say. If you are selling, then write out a document using the 8-step framework from earlier in the book. Having a script like this will also stop you from saying 'umm' and 'errr' quite as much.
2. **Use an autocue**. If you've ever watched one of my videos where I'm talking to the camera and thought it was impressive how I reeled off so

much information so concisely…well, I'm sorry to say, it wasn't actually that impressive. I don't have a perfect memory. I was using an autocue.

The good news is you can do it too. Search on your phone's app store for a free autocue app. There are plenty available. They float over the screen as you are recording. You can set the speed of the scrolling text to whatever is comfortable and away you go. It's simple and means you can get your message across quickly, concisely and professionally.

3. **Frame the video properly.** When I'm talking to the camera, I like to make sure my full torso is in shot. I use my hands a lot when I talk. Some say too much! However, it helps me to get across my enthusiasm for whatever I'm selling. So, when I frame a video, I like to make sure my torso is in shot. Anything closer seems too close and makes your hands seem massive when you reach towards the camera. And anything further away can make the viewer strain their eyes.

Also, make sure your head is in the middle of the shot. You don't want a massive gap between your head and the ceiling. And finally, try to get the actual lens of the camera at your eye level. Looking up or down at the camera makes you look weird and distorted.

4. **Get used to having to record the same thing over and over.** Recording video of yourself is

tough. It can easily take 10 attempts to make a 20 second video. You'll often stumble over your words and forget what you were going to say. Having a script helps this, but it will still happen. Sometimes you fumble on the last word, sometimes you'll stumble on the first. Just don't worry about it. This is all part of the process. You will get better at it, but it won't happen overnight.

5. **Speak to the camera like you are speaking to a person**. Speaking to a camera feels odd. It can also make you nervous. So, one of the best tips I can give you is to speak to the camera like you are speaking to a person. Preferably a friend or family member. This simple mindset shift will help you relax and loosen up. It won't make you perfect, but it will help.

To begin with, you might find it easier to have someone stand behind the camera. You can then just speak to them. It'll make everything seem less wooden and more natural. However, you might personally find that embarrassing and prefer to do it in a quiet room on your own. It doesn't matter what your preference is, just know it is normal for it to feel weird, but it will get easier.

Summary

Video is one of the most powerful weapons in your advertising arsenal and as reluctant as you might be, you need to give it a go.

Not only is it powerful, but it is still criminally underused.

The reason I believe it is underused is because people are scared.

This opens the door for you to stand out and start getting noticed. So, strap on your big boy pants and give it a go.

Follow my tips and practice, practice, practice. It will get easier, and you will get better at it.

Conclusion

I hope the tips and techniques I've shared with you in this book help you to build a bigger, stronger and more profitable painting and decorating business.

The first half of the book (Chapters 1 – 10) are designed to give you all the basics for creating brilliant adverts that make you money.

The second half (Chapter 11 – 19) are individual advertising platforms. My plan being, that if you are ever stuck for some work you can quickly pick up this book and grab some techniques and ideas to get things going again.

Advertising is a tough skill to learn. But it is perhaps the most important thing to learn if your business is going to be a success.

Knowing how to create good adverts means that you know how to write concise and convincing sales copy.

Being able to write like this will help in every aspect of your business. Not just advertising.

Think about all the other times you need to convince someone using just the written word. Emailing a supplier for better payment terms. Asking a customer to make their final payment. There are loads.

These skills will come in handy more than you might think. So, don't stop here. Keep learning, improving, and doing everything you can to stand out and stay ahead of the competition.

Thank you again for reading this book. I truly hope it helps you.

Jon

ABOUT THE AUTHOR

This is the part of the book where for some reason people start talking about themselves in the third person. (I'm not going to do that)

WHO AM I?

I started in sales in 2006. Since then I've had a number of sales and marketing roles across several companies. Some of which I was very successful. Some not so much!

I began writing in 2020 primarily to help professional painters & decorators with their sales and marketing. Something that for some reason is not part of the college courses!

My other objective is to help raise the profile of the industry that I love (Painting & Decorating) and help tradesmen across the world get the recognition they deserve.

SO WHY LISTEN TO WHAT I HAVE TO SAY?

Well, since I started in sales, I have consumed 1,000's of hours of content on the subject. I've read hundreds of books, listened to countless podcasts and been on more boring sales courses than I can remember.

Most importantly, it's been my full-time job for over 10 years. Which means I've made a hell of a lot of mistakes. All of which I have learned from and used to improve.

Even if you are a more successful salesperson than me, it doesn't mean I can't help you. After all, even Tiger Woods has a coach.

MORE INFO

For more information on me and loads of free sales and marketing tips, check out my website: www.jmears.co.uk/

To see my other books, (Including 'Sales & Marketing for Decorators) have a look at my Amazon author page: https://www.amazon.co.uk/Mr-Jon-Mears/e/B08LHDN1DD?ref_=dbs_p_ebk_r00_abau_000000

GET IN TOUCH

Email: jonmearsblogs@gmail.com

Twitter: @JonMears10

Instagram: @jmears.co.uk

Facebook: facebook.com/jmears.co.uk

Facebook group: Search – 'Sales & Marketing support for painters and decorators'

YouTube Channel name: 'Sales & Marketing for Decorators'

LinkedIn: linkedin.com/in/jon-mears/

Printed in Great Britain
by Amazon